Henry Richards

Letters of Captain Henry Richards of the Ninety-Third Ohio

Infantry

Henry Richards

Letters of Captain Henry Richards of the Ninety-Third Ohio Infantry

ISBN/EAN: 9783337091545

Printed in Europe, USA, Canada, Australia, Japan

Cover: Foto ©Andreas Hilbeck / pixelio.de

More available books at **www.hansebooks.com**

HENRY RICHARDS.

LETTERS

— OF —

CAPTAIN HENRY RICHARDS,

OF THE

NINETY-THIRD OHIO INFANTRY.

PRESS OF WRIGHTSON & COMPANY,
12 West Fourth Street, Cincinnati, O.
1883.

INTRODUCTORY.

The following letters of Captain Henry Richards, of the Ninety-third Ohio Volunteers, are compiled and published for the sake of preserving, amongst his many friends, a memento of one who was dearly loved by all who knew him, as also from a feeling of respect and esteem for his manly virtues, self-devotion and true patriotism; and, further, as the means of rendering a slight tribute through him (who was only "one of the many") to the virtues and heroism of the common soldiers of the late war, who, leaving homes and friends, and in many cases a prosperous business and brilliant future, entered voluntarily and from a simple sense of duty and love of country into a service which they well knew was full of the severest hardships and danger, and willingly, and even cheerfully, submitted to the severe discipline of the camp, subordinate frequently to men of inferior capacity to themselves, but whom they obeyed, knowing that upon that obedience and discipline the life of the army depended. These letters present a vivid picture of the life of the common soldier, for though Captain Richards did not serve as a common soldier, he shared all their hardships and duties. One of the most unselfish of men, he refused the promotion as captain of another company when offered him, feeling that he should stay with his company who were, at home, his neighbors and friends, and could not bear the idea of leaving them to be cared for by any other officer, and it was only when he found that he would serve most of his time on detached duty that he consented to be made captain of his own company.

3

Captain Richards was born September 5th, 1823, and was the eldest son of Giles Richards, Esq., who, for many years, was a prominent citizen of Butler county. He, connected with T. S. Goodman, of Cincinnati, built and operated in 1822 one of the first cotton mills of Ohio, known as the "Colerain Cotton Mills," at Colerain, Hamilton county, Ohio. Accumulating a competency, he subsequently purchased a farm in the immediate neighborhood in Butler county, where he resided until his death in 1876, devoting his time and attention to agricultural pursuits. Henry, his son, was brought up on this farm, obtaining his education at Cary's Academy, College Hill, and was engaged in farming at the breaking out of the Rebellion.

In connection with Robert Joyce, now Major Joyce, of the Internal Revenue Department, and Isaac R. Anderson, of Ross township, Butler county, he organized a company in his immediate neighborhood, which was mustered into service at Dayton, July 30th, 1862, and formed part of the Ninety-third Ohio, commanded by Colonel Charles Anderson, Robert Joyce becoming captain, and Henry Richards first lieutenant.

These letters, mostly written to his father, were carefully preserved by him and filed away amongst other letters as was his habit, and it has only been within the present year that the compiler was aware of their existence. They were found when casually looking over a mass of old letters.

A. W. G.

Elland, O., *May*, 1883.

LETTERS.

Dear Father :

I only have time to say a few words. We left Dayton Saturday about 5 p. m. The privates were all paid off, bounty and all, just as the Governor had promised. The labor of making out the three different pay-rolls and one muster-roll was immense, considering the time for doing it, and the work principally fell on me. We were the only company that were paid all at once. We arrived at Cincinnati about midnight, and were marched to Covington, arriving there about 2 a. m. We laid down on the board piles, cars, mother earth, and wherever we pleased, without supper, and had to get our breakfast as we could. Left Covington about 1 p. m. and arrived at Lexington about two to day, having eaten nothing all day; arrived at our present camp about 8 p. m. were ordered to lay down on the sides of the turnpike, with a stone for a pillow, although there was a beautiful grove on either side of the pike. We had not laid down more than an hour when there was an alarm, one of the pickets having been shot at not more than fifty yards from our company. I imagine it was done to impress upon our men the necessity of being prepared, and, if so, it had the desired effect. I lay asleep about six feet from Col. Anderson, and was on my feet about the third report of the sentinels. It was very amusing to see the effects of this first alarm on our men. Some did not know which end was up—others cool and ready for any emergency, which I did not fail to observe, being—although I say it myself—perfectly cool.

Considering the alarm of the citizens here, on account of the defeat of Mitchell, only about twenty miles from here, yesterday morning I think our men behaved very well.

5

Should our men meet with any disaster here, our State authorities I think will be very much to blame for sending such a new-born regiment into the field only partly equipped; but we are soldiers now, in earnest, and for my part I don't expect anything but a hard life; the contrary would be a disappointment to me; but the men had no reason to expect such a breaking in as they have had at the very commencement. Your son HENRY,

Co. F., 93d Ohio Infantry.

Baggage not here and no ink in camp.

CAMP CHEERFUL, September 4th, 1862.

DEAR FATHER:

I have a few moments, while the wagon-train is getting in position, to write a few lines. I call this Camp Cheerful because the men are so cheerful this morning, last night being the first night's rest and the first meal of cooked victuals we have eat since last Saturday noon. We were ordered last Saturday to prepare two days' rations, expecting to go to Camp Dick Robinson. About the time for starting the orders were changed and we took up our line of march for Richmond. We left camp after dark, and marched sixteen miles by daylight Sunday morning. During our march the latter part of the night we met many stragglers from the battle-field of Richmond. A little after daylight we halted on the hills of the Kentucky river, and sent out one company as pickets. We had not been encamped more than half an hour until we saw the enemy on the opposite side of the river on the hills in large force. We were immediately ordered back to Lexington, having rested only about two hours, and arrived there about 10 o'clock at night. It having rained very hard during our march we were not in a very good humor when we were ordered to countermarch two and one-half miles to the farm of James B. Clay, where we arrived about midnight, as wet as drowned rats, and with nothing but mother earth to sleep upon. On Monday morning the baggage wagons were ordered to unload everything but the provisions and cooking utensils. Officers and men to take a change of clothing and prepare for a march. Officers' baggage to be sent to Lexington and stored. In less than an hour we were ordered to form in line of battle, and while we were forming some one told me our baggage was ordered to be burned. I left the ranks and went to see, but it was too late—everything was piled up and on fire. Commissary stores, colonels', captains' and doctors' baggage—everything belonging to the regiment except what was on our backs was burned. This is a fair specimen of the way things are managed here. The teams went away not heavily loaded—could just as well have taken everything as not. After forming in line of battle we marched at quick time to a corn field on the farm of Henry Clay, and waited for the enemy about two hours, when orders came to retreat towards Frankfort. We marched all night; rested one hour about daylight, and resumed our march, arriving at Frankfort after dark, where we were turned into a filthy lot—without anything to eat but hard bread—to rest our weary limbs.

A little after midnight we were aroused and on our way to Louisville, distant fifty-two miles, where we are at present.

September 5th, 12 M., my birthday, by the way. This march has been conducted in the most unchristian and inhuman manner. Including cavalry and infantry we had some 10,000 men, capable of making a good fight if they had been allowed the privilege. There is a great lack of courage or capacity in this department. In fact, it is most miserably conducted from beginning to end. Colonel Anderson has been acting brigadier-general, and is sick at present. If he leaves the regiment it will be its death blow, as he is the only field officer having the confidence of the men. No more at present from your loving son,   HENRY.

CRAB ORCHARD, October 16th, 1862.

DEAR FATHER:

I have just learned that a messenger is going to Lexington in about twenty minutes and hasten to drop you a line. I wrote to sister Ellen from Shelbyville. Since then we have been on the march, with more or less skirmishing in front and rear, pursuing the rebels. Their army is now one day's march from us, in full retreat, with, I think, a fair prospect of capturing them. Had the fight at Perryville been delayed as Buell, I learned, intended, they would have been bagged there, as several divisions, including ours, were but one day's march behind. We have an immense army here now, sufficient to gobble up all the rebels if caught. We camped on the battlefield on Saturday night. The battle was fought on Wednesday. The rebel dead were still unburied, hundreds of them I saw black and stiff, most all shot in the head or breast. Our forces were only about 17,-000 while theirs are estimated much larger. They left in the night with about three thousand wounded, which were left at Harrodsburg, and our forces took them prisoners. Now our faces are toward Cumberland Gap, and if the enemy continue in that direction will follow them on. I will write more at length the first good opportunity, as the messenger is ready to go. Your affectionate son,

HENRY.

P. S.—General Sill is our division commander, and General Buckley our brigade commander. Any letter sent should be directed to Louisville, Ky., McCook's Army Corps, 2d Division, 4th Brigade, 93d Ohio Infantry.

————

LEBANON, KY., October 22d, 1862.

DEAR FATHER:

I wrote you from Crab Orchard, and was detailed the same day to come here with a train of wagons (our quartermaster being sick) after tents and knapsacks that were left behind expecting to find them here night before last, but the railroad is not yet in operation—the first train will arrive to-day. I was instructed to remain here until they come. I learn from parties who left Crab Orchard one day later than I, that Rosseau's Division and McCook's Army Corps are marching this way, but where going is not known, —we think Nashville. There is great complaint among officers and men of General Buell. Traitor is not an uncommon epithet used in connection with his name. It does seem as if the whole rebel army could have been captured or annihilated at Perryville, if he had wished it. The army suffers greatly for water, having had no rain in this country for about three months. I have been obliged to take my train six miles from town for water.

The army is dependent on the railroad for supplies, and no trains having run for several days we are consequently short of rations. There are probably five hundred wagons here waiting for supplies.

I hope Ohio may be spared the infliction of a hostile army passing through her territory. You can have no idea of the appearance of the country after an army of fifty thousand men have passed through. Fences and crops destroyed in many places, cavalry horses quartered in the front yards and fastened to the small trees and shrubbery.

I am very glad to hear of Vallan ligham's defeat. Our regiment was polled on election day. Schenck received over four hundred votes, and Val less than one hundred. Your affectionate son,

HENRY.

NASHVILLE, TENN., November 9th, 1862.

DEAR FATHER:

When I wrote you last I believe I was at Lebanon, Ky., waiting for knapsacks belonging to our regiment. They came to hand in much better order than I could have expected, and I caught up with the regiment one day's march short of Bowling Green.

We halted there two days, close to a stream known as Lost River. It comes from the ground sufficiently strong to drive two run of large mill stones, and flows about a quarter of a mile and disappears in a cave, which some of our boys penetrated a distance of a mile or more. I was ordered to make out pay rolls, which prevented me from making any explorations.

We left for Nashville on the 3d of November, and arrived here the 7th. The march was hard and dusty as usual, but water was in plenty for quenching our thirst. We are now encamped on the bank of the Cumberland River, about one and one-half miles from town.

I have not been in the city yet, and don't know when I shall, as I am entirely too *democratic* to go through the necessary forms to get there, and yet will not violate the orders. None of the officers of this company have ever asked for or had a pass to go through the lines since we have been in the service, and I believe they, like myself, have no inclination to gad about over the country at every stopping place. We are all disgusted with the country and people, and don't wish to see any more of it or them than we are obliged to in the course of our duty.

After resting one day, our brigade was ordered this morning to take the back track two days' march to Franklin, near the State line, to guard our division supply train, the Louisville & Nashville Railroad being in operation to that point, and Nashville is almost destitute of the common necessaries of life. Coffee, sugar and soap would bring almost any price asked, the citizens having been without either for two or three months. Potatoes bring one dollar per peck, and other vegetables in proportion.

Yesterday a court martial was ordered by General Sill for the division, and as I was detailed as one of that "honorable" body, I am left behind the regiment, which don't *spite* me a bit, as I don't like to go over the same ground in this country twice. I will not be called on for any other duty during its session, the length of which is uncertain; it may continue only two or three days and it may last as many weeks or months, as there are said to be a good many cases.

It seems to me our regiment ought to take the place of the Sixty-ninth, and it ought to go into more active service, as it has had ample time to drill, but it seems that the powers that be take very little thought of the rank and file. The most of the boys belonging to the Sixty-ninth from our neighborhood have been over here to see us. Wilson is not very well, having rheumatism. Parker is very well. Huey and Ogg are both fit for duty. Their regiment has not been paid off for six months, and the boys seem very anxious to get their pay and send it home. No more at present from your affectionate son,   HENRY.

BATTLEFIELD STONE RIVER, January 4th, 1863.
DEAR FATHER:

I take the first opportunity to let you know that I have passed through the dangers of the last six days without receiving a single scratch, except through my clothes.

We left Nashville on the 26th of December, in rear of the three divisions that were to advance on Murfreesboro, constituting the right wing. The advance had a good deal of skirmishing on that day. The next day we had the advance and the skirmishing was quite heavy, but we were not deployed as skirmishers, and consequently did not get a sight of the rebels until near night, when a few volleys set them running. It was a terrible day, raining almost incessantly, and we were without tents. The next day being Sunday, and the enemy having skedaddled, we rested.

Monday morning found us on the march for this place, arriving in time to give the rebels one volley by way of introduction. We encamped in a very thick wood, and slept on the ground as usual, and were in line of battle at daylight. We had hardly formed when the ball opened immediately in our front. The regiments stationed there were surprised, it seems, and gave way in disorder, retreating through our lines in great confusion. They were old regiments, too, and we expected better things of them. Our regiment took the panic and followed suit. To have tried to make a stand just then would have been folly, after three or four regiments and Willich's brigade and the Iowa batteries had been forced to retreat.

On came the rebels shouting like devils, drunk with the excitement of victory, but their tune soon changed. Rosseau's Division came promptly to our assistance, and we soon checked their advance but it cost many lives. The fighting now became very severe all along the lines. The rebs made another and another desperate attempt to drive us, but of no avail. Our men were as obstinate as they.

At night we had resisted every attempt to drive us back, and the position of affairs was rather in our favor, but the slaughter was terrible. Had not General Johnson allowed himself to be surprised the result would have been very different.

Our regiment, after Rosseau came up, was not in the engagement, although they were subject to a very heavy fire during their retreat. Colonel Anderson was slightly wounded, and Major Martin seriously. Two of our company were wounded in the fight; ten are missing, amongst them are Alexander Johnson and A. Pickens.

When our regiment was rallied Captain Joyce, Captain Birch and myself became detached from the regiment and formed ourselves with about thirty men, ten or twelve of our own company and the balance parts of different companies. The Twenty-fourth Ohio was reforming—it also having been badly scattered, when the major of the Twenty-fourth rode up and asked, "What regiment do you belong to?" We answered, "the Ninety-third Ohio." Said he, "do you want to fight? If so, form with us and show what you can do." We did so, and advanced in an open field to within range of the enemy, who opened a desperate fire upon us, which we returned with interest. We held our ground, although the enemy seemed to be far superior in numbers, for two hours, and under an incessant fire of shell and musketry that seemed to make the very earth shake. You can judge something of its fury when I tell you that our men fired seventy-three rounds during the engagement here. I never expected to get through alive, but am safe and sound, as is also Captains Joyce and Birch.

William Ogg was shot dead while carrying Richard D. Shaw off the field badly wounded. W. P. Lane also killed, also G. B. Kunler, all of our company.

The hardest fighting during the day was at this point. How any of us escaped appears a miracle. The colonel and major of the Twenty-fourth Ohio were both killed. They were brave, honest men, and were everywhere during the fight, encouraging and urging the men and their very presence was assurance of victory. I never learned their names. Since the fight of that day no one could visit the field, as it lay between the two armies, and a bone of contention until last night. A charge was made after dark when the rebs were completely routed, and the news to day is that they have evacuated the place. There has been heavy fighting every day, always in our favor.

Mrs. McNeil's boys are both well.

January 5th. We found another dead man of our company to day —Swain Car on.

The rebels have gone, and our army follows in pursuit. They have Leen badly whipped. What our next step will be I don't know. Rations are scarce here. We had two ears of corn to each man issued on Friday last, that being all that could be got. We have neither blankets nor tents. It has rained two nights since we have been here, and no fires are allowed. So you see soldiering is no play. I am very well, however; not even a cold. We lost all our blankets the first day's fight. No more paper, so must stop. As ever, your affectionate son,   HENRY.

CAMP DRAKE, April 13th, 1863.

DEAR FATHER :

I enclose forty dollars, and would send more but fear its safety, as the rebels are continually making raids upon the roads * * * Yesterday we were ordered to strike our Sibley tents and take shelter tents, which looks like preparing to move. I pay no attention to rumors but judge from appearances for myself.　　　HENRY.

___

CAMP DRAKE, April 16th, 1863.

DEAR FATHER:

A few days since I sent you forty dollars, and as we are ordered to go to Salem to morrow with four days' rations, I enclose forty dollars more. Salem is only about four miles from here, and one brigade goes out at a time to do picket duty. Your affectionate son,　　　HENRY.

___

CAMP DRAKE, TENN., June 8th, 1863.

DEAR FATHER:

We were paid off yesterday, and as our sutler is going to Nashville to-day I will get him to procure a draft on Cincinnati for the amount I send home. The only risk will be between here and Nashville.

I send $100 belonging to me.
I send　15 belonging to Amos McNeil.
I send　15 belonging to John McNeill.
I send　30 belonging to Thos. Dungan.
I send　60 belonging to Joseph Waltz.
____
Total, $220

McNeills' you can pay to their father: Thos. Dungan's to his wife; Joseph Waltz's to his wife; he is an acquaintance of C. Sick's.

We are receiving large reinforcements of paroled prisoners. I received a letter from Charley* yesterday. He is with the Thirty-ninth Ohio at Memphis. Appearances here look towards an early movement. Your aff.ctionate son,　　　HENRY.

* A cousin.

CAMP DRAKE, June 14th, 1863.

DEAR FATHER:

Enclosed find photos of the Corps Commanders of the Army of the Cumberland now here, also General Rosecrans. I wish I could have had a front view of him. We like him very much. I expected to send one of my own, but it got spoiled in printing. General McCook don't look to be equal to the position he holds; he seems to have drawn a lucky card.

I would like your opinion of the photos and men. Hoping to hear from you soon, I remain your affectionate son, HENRY.

CAMP DRAKE, June 23d, 1863.

DEAR FATHER:

We have marching orders for to-morrow with twelve days' rations, but have not the most remote idea where bound. Company H, of our regiment, being without an officer, I have been put in command of it, and if I consent to a promotion will be made captain of that company. I would much rather remain first lieutenant of my own company than be captain of any other, but I see that I will, in all probability, be on duty away from my own company most of the time, and have partly concluded to accept promotion. I received yours of the 14th, for which I am much obliged.

June 24th, 4 A. M. — We are ordered to march at 6. A. M., with baggage and transportation. If we go to the front you will hear of us soon, unless the rebels skedaddle. Will write when an opportunity offers. Your affectionate son, HENRY.

CAMP ON DUCK RIVER,
NEAR MANCHESTER, TENN., June 30th, 1863.

DEAR SISTER:

We left Murfreesboro on Wednesday, June 24th, under orders to take and hold what is known as Liberty Gap, a pass in the range of hills between Manchester and Shelbyville. Near Bell Buckle we found a brigade of rebels to dispute our passage, which ought to have been sufficient to have held us in check, considering their position; but after heavy skirmishing, amounting almost to a battle, in which ours and Davis' division lost about two hundred killed and wounded, they were driven out. This occupied the 24th and 25th.

During this time it rained almost incessantly, which made it impossible to get our transportation through. As the main battle, if any, was expected at Hoover's Gap, on this road, we were ordered to make a night march to reinforce Crittenden and Thomas; which we did in mud often knee-deep, wading a creek seventeen times during the night, camping about 1 o'clock with no covering but rubber blankets, and raining in torrents. With a rail for a pillow and a bundle of wheat for a bed, I slept as soundly as I ever did.

We were on our way by half past four in the morning; arrived at Hoover's Gap about 3 P. M., and found Hardee's Corps had been driven after severe skirmi-hing. Here Crittenden's Corps moved toward Shelbyville. Thomas on this road—McCook's Corps to follow him. We were ordered to take three days' rations and march at 4 A. M. on the 28th. The roads were impassable, or would be considered so by any other army, and our train did not get in motion till noon. Our division was the rear guard. We were ordered to make this point, but after floundering through the mud and rain until 2 A. M. of the 29th, we were brought to a dead halt during one of the most terrific thunder storms I ever experienced.

If you had seen the Second Army Corps at this time you might have realized what soldiering is. In five minutes every man was lying down in the mud and water, and in five minutes more were sleeping as soundly as though at home. Perhaps you may doubt this, but it is certainly true, for I being in command of Company H, was called on to furnish men for picket, and did not find one man awake. They were so completely exhausted that many of them fell asleep in a sitting posture. We were on the march again by daylight, and arrived here about 8 A. M. The rain continued to fall in torrents until last night. Yesterday all knapsacks and baggage not actually needed, were ordered to be sent back. The men were not allowed to carry more than "one blanket, either woolen or rubber." All chose the rubber, and you may rest assured that many a poor fellow in this army has reason to bless the one who introduced them.

Each company was ordered to carry two axes, two spades and one pick, and be reduced to one-half rations of bread, and be ready to march at a moment's notice. This morning it is reported that we are stuck in the mud, which I think is very likely, but one day's sunshine will put us in motion again. There is a gigantic effort being made to clear this State of rebels, but the weather may retard our progress. My opinion is that they are skedaddling in every direction. There is a report in camp that no letters will be allowed to leave Murfreesboro for fifteen days. There has been a continued storm during the last five days. Rubber blankets keep our shoulders dry, but at night the side next the ground gets wet. Our feet have not been dry a moment, and the mud has no bottom.

Many have lost their shoes or worn them out, and yet at sick call this morning not a single man from my company answered it, although they could have been sent back if not considered fit for field duty. Their trials and hardships are borne with scarcely a murmur.

It seems to me that such men can never go to a very bad place; at least, I have a better opinion of the Ruler of all things than to suppose they will not be rewarded for their devotion to their country. My health was never better. I feel as well this morning as I could wish. I think I have written you several letters that you have never received; one in particular, with a butternut letter enclosed, that one of our men received, as you have never mentioned it. Postboy waits. Good-bye for the present. Your brother,

HENRY.

——

TULLAHOMA, July 4th, 1863.

DEAR MOTHER :

I wrote you a few lines from Duck River, also a letter to sister Elizabeth. We left our camp on Duck River on the 1st July about 10 A. M., the roads almost impassable in places even for infantry. We were delayed by teams and artillery so much that we did not arrive here until after midnight. The rebels commenced evacuating this place the night before about midnight. They were said to have been 30,000 strong, and left in such a hurry as to leave tents standing, which come very convenient to us, as ours were all thrown away or sent back. I am now writing in a tent marked "Alabama Penitentiary !" It is a poor one but better than

none. We are now preparing the ground for a permanent camp. It is said we are to remain here to hold this point.   *   *   *
General Rosecrans' headquarters are here. He keeps with the army, and consequently knows everything that transpires. He has a movable telegraph which follows the advance, and as fast as he comes up it is taken up and follows him. I was on picket yesterday and saw them taking it up within an hour after he passed. There is a party at each end, one to pull down, the other to put up. They use light poles through cleared land and fasten it to branches of trees in the woods, and it is put up very rapidly.

Our baggage arrived here yesterday; everything saturated with water—my valise almost ruined. It has rained every day since we left Murfreesboro, and such rains I never saw before. I put on my first washing this morning—pants, shirts, socks, handkerchiefs and towels, all washed in cold water without soap. They don't look remarkably white, but they are cleaner than they were. There has been many times on this march that I had wished folks at home could have seen us. They can form but little idea of our appearance. I walked through our camp the night we arrived. The men were tired and worn out, and just dropped down on the ground and were asleep immediately. The peaceful looking moon was shining, O! so brightly, and their haggard and care-worn countenances, as they lay asleep, showed plainly what they had gone through. Their courage and endurance is wonderful. * * *
As ever, your affectionate son,   HENRY.

CAMP VON TREBA,
NEAR BELLEFONTE, August 29th, 1863.

DEAR FATHER:

I have not written you since we left Camp Reed, and will now endeavor to give you a short description of our march here. We left camp Sunday at 3 P. M., August 16th, with only about one hour's notice, with ten days' rations. The weather was very hot, but as usual when we start on a march it commenced to rain, which made slippery and muddy marching, but it cleared off next day and we were free from dust.

2

Our camp Sunday night was on Elk River, seven miles from Tullahoma. The next day we marched through Manchester and camped five miles beyond. The next day's march of twenty-five miles was very severe, owing to the heat, and we reached the foot of the Cumberland Mountains, on Hurricane Fork, but owing to our having to diverge from our route, by reason of a pontoon train blocking up the road, over the mountain, night found us no nearer Bellefonte, our point of destination, than when we started in the morning, with a much worse road to cross. To the top of the mountain it was about 2400 yards, and the elevation about 800 yards, and we were ordered to reach Bellefonte by Thursday, but we were just two days getting our trains to the top of the mountain, it requiring ten mules and fifteen or twenty men to get a single wagon along the road. Such cutting, slashing and swearing I think never could have been heard before or since. It was between Winchester and the mountains that Colonel McCook was murdered last summer, and very little restraint was put upon the men while in that neighborhood. A very large farm at the foot of the mountain, where the division lay while the teams were climbing the road, was completely shorn of everything—not an ear of corn, peach nor apple, of which there was an abundance, was left. The old man, owner of the place, had some ten or fifteen hives of bees which were all taken and the contents appropriated in short order, also chickens, turkeys, geese and everything that could be eaten. There are, no doubt, many who would say all rebels should be treated this way by our army, but could they see the demoralizing effects of such a course upon the men they would be satisfied it was the worst policy that could be pursued. Men must be restrained by severe discipline in an army or they will soon run into excesses that will render them totally unfit for duty. The desire for plunder, tear down and destroy, is one of the most degrading instincts of our nature, and will soon destroy the usefulness of the best of troops.

After arriving on the top of the mountain we had a pleasant, sandy and shady road. At every halt the men would go out in the woods in search of rattlesnakes, which seemed the principal production of the country, and were killed in great numbers, within a few feet of the road.

The inhabitants of these mountain regions seem very ignorant, especially the women, who all chew tobacco and dip snuff. I asked one woman how far it was to the next town. She did not know; she had never *hearn* tell. Another did not know the name of the creek she was living by. She "had *hearn* it called a *creek* but never *hearn* no name for it."

On Sunday night we camped on top of the mountain, and arrived here Saturday the 22d. We are about a quarter of a mile from the town of Bellefonte, a poor looking and dilapidated place. The citizens all leave about this time of the year, it is said, on account of sickness of the locality—fevers seem to prevail. The Tennessee River is about half a mile from our camp, with very high hills on the opposite side. We are in a valley, and have very heavy fogs and quite cool nights. Our camp is very pleasant. The men have taken great pains to make themselves comfortable, General Johnson allowing them to tear down about half the town and pick up all loose boards, and those that are not loose soon become so; and they have built comfortable bunks, and with the aid of grass and cedar boughs they are very comfortably fixed. The grounds are kept very clean, 'and fires are built night and morning to keep off the damp.

Deserters are constantly coming within our lines.

There seems considerable corn growing, though I don't think there is much prospect of the rebels harvesting it.

Your son,   HENRY.

P. S. Sunday, August 30th. We are ordered to March at 7 o'clock this morning. Don't know where.   H.

DE KALB COUNTY, ALABAMA,
NEAR THE GEORGIA LINE, September 4th, 1863.

DEAR FATHER:

I wrote you the morning we left Camp Von Treba, and, as we will lay here until noon, will write you a few lines. We marched to within a short distance of Stephenson, Alabama, where we crossed the Tennessee on pontoons. It was about four hundred yards wide, and took fifty-seven pontoons, and was put across in four hours. We camped about a mile from the river, at the foot of the mountain, on Monday night, and laid there until Wednesday morning for other troops to cross. It took all of Wednesday to get one train up the mountain. Yesterday we were rear-guard of our division, and had a very hard day's march, not starting until nearly noon, and making about fifteen miles, the dust shoe-mouth deep. When we left Camp Von Treba our destination was Trenton, Georgia, and that may be our point yet, but our course yesterday was nearly south, a little east, which would indicate some other point; but it may be necessary to go in this direction to get around some mountain or other obstacle. We had another reduction of baggage at the foot of the mountain, and now only three wagons are allowed to a regiment, and we are evidently going to penetrate Georgia, perhaps to flank Chattanooga, where the Rebs are said to be working night and day on the fortifications. Nothing seems to indicate a probability of our defeat, else such extensive trains as we have would have been left on the other side of the Tennessee. The entire army must be south of that river. One-half of the railroad bridge at Bridgeport was destroyed, and will have to be rebuilt before we can go very far.

If we can get possession of the road leading to Atlanta, they will have to whip Rosecrans, or their entire army will be captured or scattered. If they allow us to flank them, and then make a stand, the fight will be desperate; but they must be in a desperate strait, though they are fifty thousand strong, as we learn. The recent castigations they have had must surely dishearten them. We find everything deserted as we march along, and I don't wonder much, for nothing but destruction marks our path, and I am sorry to say that occasional acts are perpetrated that only fiends could be guilty of. It is a great misfortune to live in the track of an army.

We are without tents again, but so long as the weather remains pleasant we don't need them. They, with all extra baggage, are stored at Stephenson. The men are in good health and spirits. There is very little known of the intentions of the Commander, but it seems to me Rosecrans is massing his forces, or going to somewhere at or near Rome, Georgia.

The mail will be very uncertain for some time. This will, perhaps, not leave before day after to-morrow, but I thought I would have it ready. Hoping to hear from you soon, I am, as ever,

Your affectionate son,   HENRY.

September 5th.—We moved yesterday about four miles, and are encamped in a valley west of Lookout Mountain. Several thousand cavalry left here yesterday morning on a raid. We are about half-way between Trenton and Lebanon. I have just thought that this is my birthday; forty years old—past the average of human life! I have seen enough confusion during the past year, and I feel like ending the balance of my life in quiet. This kind of life I fear will have the opposite effect on very many who have been leading a soldier's life, and I sometimes fear for the consequences when the army is disbanded after this war is over. It seems now that nothing but the strictest military regulations can control them.

HENRY.

CHATTANOOGA, September 22d, 1863.

DEAR FATHER:

The events of the last few days have been so exciting and frought with so many events of interest, that I hardly know where to begin, and I have forgotten when and where I last wrote you, but believe it was at the foot of Lookout Mountain. Since then, until last Thursday evening, when we joined the main army, we were marching and counter-marching among the mountains, seeking an outlet by which we could join the main body on Chickamauga Creek. We came off the mountains Thursday afternoon, and went into camp about dark, after a march of nearly thirty miles. Next morning we were sent to the front, and placed upon picket within a few hundred yards of the enemy's pickets. There were occasional shots during the day and night exchanged by the pickets, without any injury, on our side at least. On Saturday morning, there not being any considerable force in our front, we were moved to a position near the left of our line of battle. Fighting had commenced before we got our position, which was about noon. In half an hour our brigade was engaged, the Fifth Kentucky and First Ohio in advance, the Ninety-third and Sixth Indiana supporting them. We had driven the enemy about a mile, when they attacked the Fifth Kentucky on the left flank, and we immediately went to their relief and were hotly engaged for about two hours, when they gave back. Our ammunition was nearly exhausted, and I was sent back for a supply. During my absence our regiment made temporary breastworks of logs. Our cartridge boxes were hardly replenished when we heard the enemy's cry of "forward, double-quick!" They came on with a rush, and we poured in a galling fire which checked them for a moment, but another line coming immediately behind, pressed us so hard that we were forced back a short distance. It was during this charge that Colonel Strong was wounded in the shoulder, and was carried off the field. Colonel Baldwin, our brigade commander, came up at this moment, and seeing our wavering condition and our colonel wounded, grasped our colors and shouted "forward!" and the men, taking up the shout, charged with such determination that the rebs were forced to give way, and we pursued them about two hundred yards beyond our breast-works and captured two pieces of artillery.

They had another double line immediately in our front which we did not consider prudent to attack, and fell back to our breast-works. We lay there until nearly sundown, when they attacked us with, as I thought, fresh troops. We held our position until dark, when we fell back, they following us, and the fighting continued until after dark. One of our guns became entangled in the underbrush and trees—it all being in heavy timber—and we lost it. Both parties now retired for the night. After dark our men became a good deal scattered. We had ten killed and some sixty wounded in the day's fight, quite a number missing. Next morning—Sunday—the Ninety-third could muster about one hundred and twenty men for duty. We built breastworks again of logs, which proved of great service during the day. About 9 o'clock the ball opened again in earnest, and raged with unparalleled fury until noon. Our regiment and brigade held their position firmly. From noon until 3 o'clock we could distinctly hear the rebel officers urging their men forward, but they could not be induced to face what they knew they could not drive.

The fighting on the right and left was now terrific. Our forces on the left were forced back; the right was also giving way, and this completely cut us off.

Colonel Berry now ordered the First Ohio and Fifth Kentucky to attack the flank of the enemy that were driving our left, which they did, and opened a way for our retreat, which was made without pursuit, although we had to pass a cross-fire of shot and shell that was furious.

Our brigade and division is highly complimented for its fighting qualities. General Johnson has reason to be proud of it. Never did men hold their position with more tenacity, but I know also that other divisions did as well. The rebels were not in a condition to follow. In our front they must have lost largely. We suffered but little—thanks to our breastworks; only one man killed and fifteen wounded during Sunday.

For some days previous to the fight I had been quite unwell, and but for the reflections that are almost sure to be cast upon an officer who is absent from his command at the critical moment, I would have gone to the hospital at Stephenson, some days before. I was not able to walk, and had been riding on the ambulance for three or four days. The excitement gave me strength, however, and I went through the first day tolerably well, but the second day my energies seemed to desert me, and I frequently found myself inclining to sleep, notwithstanding the din and roar of battle all around me. The order for retreat aroused me from my lethargy, and I made a desperate effort to escape being captured. We fell back about four miles and encamped for the night. We had scarcely anything to eat for two days, and nothing to cover us at night, although I captured a rebel blanket the first night, but was unable to carry it in the retreat.

Yesterday morning I got permission from Colonel Berry to go to the rear, and am now in the officers' hospital. A few days' rest will set me all right. I feel better to-day.

The rebels, it seems, outnumbered us very considerably. Rosecrans, I hear, did not expect to fight them until Burnside's and a portion of Grant's army arrived. Why they are not here is a query.

Our lines are near the town, and if reinforcements arrive soon, all well. Our trains are all safely over the river, and we have nothing to guard. The rebs will probably attack us again to-morrow, if not to-day, as they must know we are looking for reinforcements. A great many come into our lines and give themselves up. I don't think that the Kentucky or Tennessee troops were placed in their front lines.

Lieutenant Anderson is safe.

I have not had a change of clothing since leaving Bellefonte.

September 23d.—I am across the river with our train. Can take better care of myself here than in the hospital. Don't be alarmed about me—a few days' rest will put me all right. Your son,

HENRY.

———

OCTOBER 29th, 1863.

DEAR FATHER:

I keep so little account of time that I hardly know when I last wrote you, and the past three days have been so full of excitement and interest to our brigade, and, indeed, to the whole Army of the' Cumberland, that I have hardly thought of anything else than that which pertains to our duty here. Our brigade is composed of nine regiments, viz. : Sixth Ohio, Sixth Indiana, Fifth, Sixth and Twenty-third Kentucky, First, Forty first, Ninety-third, and One Hundred and Twenty-fourth Ohio, commanded by Brigadier General W. B. Hazen. On Sunday last we were ordered to select 125 men from our regiment, to be divided into five squads, of twenty-four men each, and one commissioned officer. Enough men were selected from the brigade to make fifty-two such squads. They were divided into two detachments; one commanded by Colonel Wylie, of the Forty-first Ohio, the other by Major Birch, of the Ninety-third Ohio, and the whole by General Hazen. The balance of the regiments were commanded by Colonel Langdon, of the First Ohio. The commanders of regiments were ordered to select those that could be most depended upon, and who had never flinched in the discharge of their duty. I had the honor to command one of the squads from our regiment. The desire to know what was going on was intense, and speculation ran high. We had been living on less than half rations for some time, and the prospect of an increase of fare looked gloomy enough. The only road to haul over was impassable almost, and the forage for the animals so scarce that they were dying like rotten sheep. The rebels held the river and two wagon roads as well as the railroad. Our supplies had to be hauled a distance of sixty miles, over very bad roads. By the roads the rebels held, twenty-eight miles hauling would only be necessary. It was surmised that an effort was to be made to open the short route to Bridgeport, and to do this it was necessary to gain the opposite or southern bank of the river, some two miles below Lookout Mountain. On Monday we organized our squads, and on Tuesday evening Colonel Langdon was ordered to get his remnants of regiments in readiness to march, as we supposed, to Bridgeport. They got started about 10 o'clock P. M. Our squads had no notice yet. I went to bed fully expecting work before morning. At midnight we were aroused and ordered to march immediately. In half an hour we were off. Our course was towards the pontoon bridge, where we soon arrived, and found fifty-two pontoon boats ready, in which we embarked, with orders to preserve the strictest silence. We had to run the blockade for a distance perhaps of four miles, land and storm a hill occupied by the enemy, some two or three hundred feet high, and almost perpendicular. It was a beautiful night, the moon almost full, which was greatly against us, and as we glided silently down the stream, no sound, save the occasional dipping of an oar, we had plenty of time for reflection, and I presume of the 1300 men in these frail boats, that a single cannon shot would sink, the reflections were much the same; home and the dear ones came in for a good share. The boat I occupied was about the center of the fleet. We were to land at separate points, about one-fourth of a mile apart. When within half a mile of our place for landing, the front boats were fired upon as they were landing, which we expected would alarm the rebel camp and subject us to a heavy fire when we attempted to land, as we knew everything depended upon our getting to the top of the bluff before daylight, and as silence was now of no use, we urged our oarsmen to pull hard and make a speedy landing, which was done with a will, and as the boats touched the land every man sprang ashore, and made for the top of the bluff as fast as possible, and this was not very fast, I assure you, the ascent being very steep and rocky. However, we gained the summit just at daylight, and found the top of the ridge hardly wide enough for two men to stand upon, and the descent, on the opposite side, just as great. The rebels, having been alarmed, were making a desperate effort to climb to the summit, but we were about five minutes ahead, and they were compelled to beat a hasty retreat by a few shots from our skirmishers. The detachment which landed below was not quite so fortunate. They had three or four killed and several wounded. We took several prisoners, and they confessed it was a complete surprise, and "a d——d Yankee trick!" The pontoons were immediately put to work ferrying over the remnants of our brigade, which had marched to the opposite bank of the river, and were ready to reinforce us. They also brought a supply of plank, and by 3 P. M., of the same day, we had a good pontoon bridge over the river, which made our position secure.

It was a daring feat, well planned and successfully carried out. We all felt much better afterwards, too. We were immediately set to work building breast-works of logs, and by 10 A. M. felt ourselves secure against any force the rebs could bring against us. We left camp without a morsel in our haversacks, but our boys soon found plenty of corn to parch, and some fat hogs and cattle which were quickly appropriated to our use. The enemy attempted to shell us out for a time, but soon gave it up. Yesterday, about 3 P. M., a shot from Lookout Mountain, which is less that three miles from us, seemed to indicate that a force was approaching from another direction, and we began to prepare for friend or foe, and our suspense was soon relieved by the appearance of the advance guard of General Hooker's eastern troops coming down the valley. At first they came very cautiously, not knowing whether we were friends or foes, but when we waved the old flag they sent up a shout that fairly made the hills shake. They camped in the valley below us, and we and they were soon mingling as only soldiers and brothers can. Their camp fires at night presented a magnificent sight as we looked at them from our heights; but they were not allowed to rest very long. About midnight the rebs attacked their pickets, and they were called to arms. The Thirty-third Massachusetts and Seventy-third Ohio made a desperate charge on the rebel works and drove them out, losing about thirty killed and about a hundred wounded, the fight lasting about three hours, and was an entire success. The men had to climb a very steep hill and force them from their works at the point of the bayonet. These two regiments deserve the highest praise for their determined bravery.

October 31st. — We are still occupying the same position as when I wrote the above. We now hold the river and road to Bridgeport, except about two miles between us and Chattanooga, where Lookout Point comes to the river. We have fitted up two old steamboats. One ran the blockade night before last, and is expected to return to our pontoon from Bridgeport to-day with rations. The

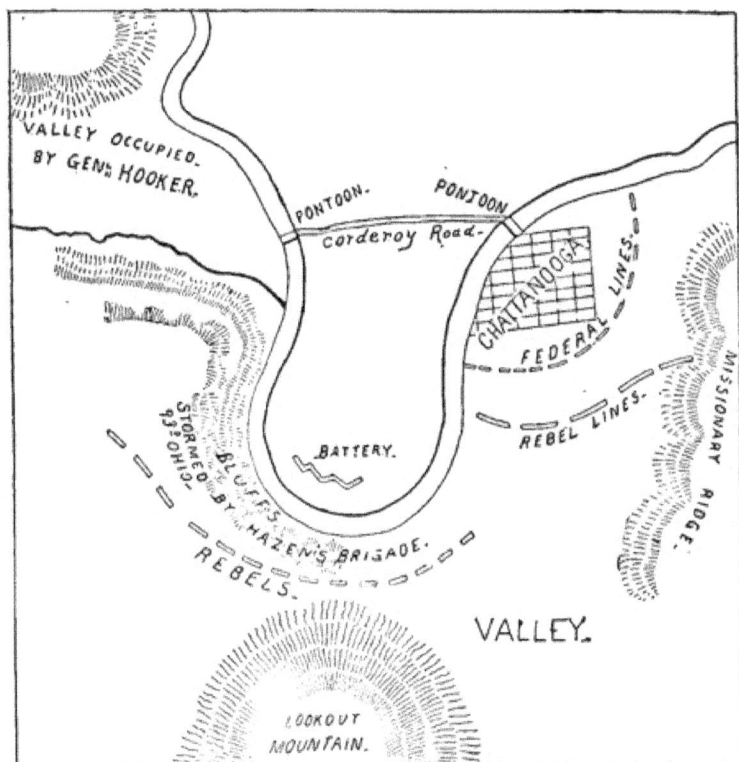

VALLEY OCCUPIED. BY GENL HOOKER.

PONTOON.

PONTOON.

Corderoy Road.

CHATTANOOGA

FEDERAL LINES.

REBEL LINES.

MISSIONARY RIDGE.

BATTERY.

BLUFFS. STORMED BY HAZEN'S BRIGADE. 93D OHIO.

REBELS.

VALLEY.

LOOKOUT MOUNTAIN.

CHATTANOOGA AND SURROUNDINGS.

other will probably be down to-night. We are building a corduroy road across the point from our pontoon to the one opposite Chatta nooga, some two or three miles, and will have a landing here which will make us independent of the blockade at Point Lookout.

Yesterday I had charge of a fatigue party at work on the road. It rained all day, but nothing short of a flood would stop work here. We have no tents with us, and it makes little difference where we are. The rain continued last night. After wringing out our blankets, we wrapped ourselves up in them and turned in. I felt quite unwell when I laid down, but I went through a steaming process under the wet blanket, and I am all right this morning. I have a prospect of going to Nashville on business for the regiment soon, and, if I do, will try to drop you a line from that point. I enclose a rough sketch of Chattanooga and surroundings. Love to all. From your affectionate son,   HENRY.

CAPITOL BUILDING,
NASHVILLE, TENN., November 14th, 1863.

DEAR FATHER:

I left Chattanooga on Tuesday last with stores for convalescents, which I left at Stephenson, and came on here on cars in search of baggage belonging to some six regiments, which was sent here to be stored last summer. I don't know how long I shall be here, but perhaps several days, as it is difficult to get transportation, and red tape unwinds slowly. When I return I shall apply for leave of absence, and come home, if possible, for a short time.

I am sitting in cousin Edward's office. He is on General Gillam's staff, pleasantly situated, I think. When you write, address me at this place, care Adjutant General's Office, and Edward will send it me. Affectionately, your son,   HENRY.

CHATTANOOGA, February 5th, 1864.

DEAR SISTER:

I arrived here yesterday, but the prospect for getting forward is not very encouraging, no person being allowed to go by boat.

Our regiment, I learn, is near Loudon.

The weather here is very beautiful now.

My anxiety about affairs at Knoxville seems to decrease as I near the place. There seems to be no alarm for that point here.

I hear that Lieutenant Isaac Anderson was wounded at the recent fight at Strawberry Plains. I sincerely hope not seriously.

I shall go forward the first opportunity.

Your affectionate brother,

HENRY.

KNOXVILLE, TENN., February 11th, 1864.

DEAR FATHER:

I wrote sister from Chattanooga, not expecting to be here so soon, but being acquainted with one of the sanitary agents at Chattanooga, and learning that they were allowed to ship thirty packages on each boat, with an agent in charge, I offered to take charge of one of the shipments so that I might get to the regiment, which I learn is at Lenoir, about six miles from Loudon, which accounts for my being here. I shall go to the regiment to morrow.

The railroad from Chattanooga to this place will be in running order in a few days, except the bridge at Loudon.

From Chattanooga to Loudon by river is 160 miles. The weather was very fine, and our trip was very pleasant. Our list of passengers consisted of Generals Schofield and Stoneman, with one aid, and Captain Sturgis, a brother of General Sturgis, a mail agent, a correspondent of the Cincinnati Commercial and myself.

I hope General Schofield will prove more efficient than General Foster has the reputation of here. The Dandridge affair seems, from the best accounts I can get, to have been a miserable scare. It seems to me our superior officers, and more especially those of the regular army, don't appreciate the courage of our citizen soldiers. Our men really want to fight, but they don't get half a chance to show what they can do. From what I have seen of our men I believe they will prove, under skillful and courageous officers, like old Zach. Taylor for instance, the best soldiers the world ever saw. We have come out here to fight and to win, and we intend to do it. I am of the opinion that after awhile, when our generals really know us, that you will see some *"tall"* fighting.

Knoxville has more the appearance of a northern town than any
town I have yet seen in the South.

No alarm is felt at present of an advance by the rebels.

Supplies are limited and will continue to be until the railroad is
finished.

Military affairs here seem to have been managed rather loosely.
The new commandant will have a good opportunity to show his
ability in securing good discipline.

Lieutenant Anderson is here. He was wounded in the skirmish
at Dandridge in his left arm. He is doing well.

I am feeling better than when I left home, though I have not
been subject lately to any great exposure. I am in hopes to be able
soon to get assigned to some duty where I shall not be expo-ed to
picket duty, as I wish to remain in the service as long as the other
boys of the regiment. As ever, your affectionate son,

HENRY.

CHATTANOOGA, February 19th, 1864.

DEAR SISTER:

Since I wrote you last, I have been to Knoxville and to the
regiment, which was encamped at Lenoir Station, on the railroad
leading from here. I found them enjoying perfect health—not a
man to attend sick call. I wish you could have seen them. They
were having good times after the hard work, and the miserable retreat from Dandridge, which was much against their wishes. Generals Hazen and Willich think it was a disgraceful affair. Had the
boys been allowed, they would have driven Longstreet from the
country. It's shameful, such affairs. The boys have left their homes
and friends to come out here to fight, and those in command won't
let them. They are not understood by those in command. Surely,
we all feel that this war can't be ended without fighting, and we
want it to begin right away. I never saw men more put out. I was
with the regiment only three days, and was ordered here to bring
up goods, and am now awaiting transportation.

Since leaving the regiment, I learned they marched the next day
after I left to Knoxville, and the report here to-day is, that heavy
fighting has been going on at Knoxville. It may only be a rumor,

however, though I am satisfied the rebs have nothing to gain by delay, and if they expect to win must strike quickly.

On the cars, coming here, were quite a number of East Tennessee and North Georgia refugees, and amongst them were two privates of the Thirty-fifth Ohio, who were taken prisoners at Chickamauga and taken to Richmond, where they were about being removed to some point in Georgia when they and several others managed to escape and made their way through the Confederacy, coming into our lines at Maysville. They were three months traveling, nearly the whole way at night, subsisting for six days at a time on corn alone. The last half of the way they found great difficulty in getting along, as they had to avoid the roads. The darkies were their only sure friends, and had they not fallen in with a Union man, named the "Red Fox," who has been engaged in piloting refugees and fugitives through the mountains ever since the beginning of the war, they would probably have been captured. This man charges everyone he brings safely through ten dollars, unless he enlists in the Union army, and if he does so enlist, he only charges two dollars! The rebs have tried in vain to catch him.

The mountains, in fact, are full of Union men fleeing from the rebel conscript. The people of East Tennessee are different from any I have seen south—much more like the northern people. More even than those of Kentucky, and as loyal generally as those of the north; but they are terribly surrounded, and I fear will suffer before this war is over. Your affectionate brother,

HENRY.

———

KNOXVILLE, March 7th, 1864.

DEAR FATHER:

I am again here where the convalescents of our brigade are in camp. The regiment, together with the balance of the Fourth, Ninth and Twenty-third Army Corps, have gone in pursuit of Longstreet, and I understand found him in position at Bull's Gap. Our brigade is near Newmarket.

There is a rumor to-day that hospital stewards and surgeons have orders to prepare supplies for a thirty-days' campaign, which looks very much like a fight. I suppose all that are able will be sent to the front, and I will be one of that number, as I am much better than I have been for several months. I am afraid Longstreet's forces are more than a match for what we can bring against him at present, but presume the generals are posted.

I don't feel as confident of this army as I did of the Army of the Cumberland; and nowhere this side of Nashville do matters seem as well managed as when Rosecrans had command. There may be better fighting generals than he, but none that I have seen are equal to him in organizing and disciplining an army and keeping his men together.

I received a letter from sister yesterday, of February 11th, the only line I have had for months. We are almost out of the world as regards news.

General Hazen has come in from the front. He thinks our division will return to Chattanooga. He leaves for Ohio to morrow.

Your son,   HENRY.

In a letter to his sister, under date of Knoxville, March 8th, he says: "Everything in this Department seems to be demoralized, and our division that has showed such good discipline is fast becoming contaminated. Oh, for such a man as Rosecrans. He is the best manager and the best calculated to keep his men together of any man I have yet seen. There was some satisfaction in being a soldier under him; but I am fast becoming disgusted with the situation of things here, but hope for the best.

My health is better than it has been since last September.

H.

CAMP NINETY-THIRD OHIO, May 3d, 1864.

DEAR FATHER:

We move at noon to day. I know nothing of the probability of a fight, but believe we move with that intention if the rebs stand.

I see by the papers that the militia of Ohio are called out for 100 days, which I suppose will give brother George a chance of soldiering. He should take nothing but what he can carry on a

march, though I suppose they will not have much of that to do.
One blanket, one extra pair socks, one extra shirt, haversack, canteen and rubber blanket, with half of a shelter tent is all he should take. The pants he wears will last him. A tin plate, knife and fork and spoon, tin-cup and very small tin bucket, with cover, that will hold about a quart, to make coffee in, a little sack for coffee, one for sugar and one for salt, just large enough to hold three days' rations, and a small frying pan completes the outfit. He will find when he carries all these with gun, cartridge-box, with forty rounds ammunition, he will have a pretty good load. Nothing is better than Government shoes for the march, and they should be one size larger than he wears at home. Thousands are doing just at this time as I am, writing to dear ones at home, not knowing but it may be the last letter, but still hopeful.

We had white frost last night and it is quite cool to day. The general call is sounding, and I must close.

With good bye, from your affectionate son,   HENRY.

CASSVILLE, GA., May 20th, 1864.

DEAR FATHER:
We have just received notice that we would remain in our present position for the day, to rest, which we very much need.

Since the rebels left Resacca we have not been out of the sound of the musketry of our skirmishers, and deserters and captured rebels have given us information that they would fight us at two or three different places.

This is the last point, and we expected warm work this morning, but they have left during the night, and a place called High Tower, on Etowa River, is now said to be the last ditch.

I, with my company, was sent out on the skirmish line yesterday about noon. The forest was very dense. The undergrowth was so thick it was almost impossible to see a man until within a few paces of him, and seems to me a line of resolute and determined men could have killed or wounded every one of us; but we drove them nearly three miles without any loss, and finally charged them across an open field with a yell, and drove them from behind a fence skirting the woods, just as night closed in. Many shots came uncomfortably close, but a miss is as good as a mile, and we are all alive and well this morning. Since the 7th of this month we have been in a state of constant excitement. Not a day has passed without bullets whistling about our heads. We were often called up at night to build breastworks, or repel a threatened attack upon some portion of our lines. Our men look haggard and worn-out. We have full rations of pork, hard bread, sugar and coffee; nothing else. We have no clothing, tents nor baggage—nothing but what we carry. and as we are obliged to carry three days' rations on our person, it makes a good load for hot weather—though the nights are cold. I still carry my overcoat but will be compelled to throw it away soon if it gets warmer. We had reason to believe, after the active winter campaign of our corps, and the easy times of the Fourteenth Corps, which were marched only to Ringgold during the winter, that they would take the advance and relieve us somewhat of the duties of an active campaign in front, but we were mistaken. I feel that, if not imposed upon, we are at least doing more than our share of the work.

The rebels are conducting their retreat very well, and are losing but little stores and not many men. I think, let them stand where they may, we are able to whip them, unless they should get large reinforcements from Richmond; and it seems to me they must give up one point or the other, and Atlanta is almost the center of their Confederacy, and only fifty-six miles from here. They take all citizens with them as they go, leaving only a few women and children behind. They must be getting pretty thick somewhere, and if we and the eastern army are successful, it seems to me the end cannot be far off.

Should this campaign end in a decided success, I think seriously of offering my resignation, and feel it, in consideration of failing health, to be my duty to do so. Your son,

HENRY.

Note.—This letter, by oversight, was left out of its proper place, and should have been placed with the 1863 letters, as the date indicates.

CAMP READ,
NEAR TULLAHOMA, TENN., July 21st, 1863.

DEAR FATHER:

I received yours and mother's of July 15th on Sunday.

We heard through the papers of the John Morgan raid and some of the particulars. I supposed he had taken my horse from Colonel Williamson's where I had left it.

I hope George was satisfied. He and Giles must have felt cheap. The idea of taking a horse and buggy to go on a scout after rebels shows a want of judgment which I would not have attributed to either of them, but it may prove a good lesson to both.

The boys out here don't feel much sorry that Morgan has paid some of their friends in Ohio and Indiana this visit. It is a little foretaste of what they may expect if they fold their hands and look on. I fear it will take about two such visits a year to rouse some of them to a proper sense of their duty. Many a wish has been made by the boys here that such and such a one might get their horses stolen and their place raided as Morgan's men know how. Should there be any more such raids don't think of leaving your home for a safer place, for there is much more respect paid to private property when the owners are about, particularly if there be women and children. If a house is deserted the soldiers are very apt to plunder, and even burn it, when the presence of a woman or child most always secure safety, and they rarely disturb peaceable citizens.

Captain Joyce has applied for leave of absence with, I think, good prospect of success, and if he goes home you will see him, I am sure.

There is a rumor in camp that our brigade will go to Decherd soon, which is some twelve mile further in advance.

The recent victories have encouraged us very much.

The weather is very warm, but we have a pleasant air stirring all the time.　　　Your affectionate son,　　　HENRY.

P. S.—I forgot to tell you before that the non commissioned officers and privates of Co. F presented me a few days since a beautiful sword, belt and sash, which I shall ever prize very highly, coming as it does from the men of another company, from the one I helped organize, and after a year's service with them.   H.

NEAR DALLAS, GA., June 3d, 1864.

DEAR FATHER:

As the mail is said to go out this evening, I use the last scrap of paper I have to say that I am well, and things are working as well, perhaps as they can be expected to. There is more or less fighting along the lines every day and night, but without anything decisive. The rebels, I think, are being punished the most, and we stick to them very close, and there are strong signs of disaffection, by frequent desertions, though during this campaign they seem more determined to fight to the last than ever before.

We are pretty well supplied with rations, the men drawing three days for four. We are all getting very dirty, having no soap and spending most of our time in the trenches. Hoping to hear from you soon, I am   Your affectionate son,

HENRY.

JUNE 6th, 1864.

DEAR FATHER:

Mail failed to bring me anything last night. Merely write to say the rebs left our front night before last, and yesterday we had an opportunity of examining the ground of the recent fight. While I am writing our forces are getting ready to march—I suppose in pursuit. Their position here was a stronger one than at Resaca. I suppose Sherman flanked them—he always does.

Your son.   HENRY.

CAMP NEAR ACKWORTH, GA., June 8th, 1864.

DEAR FATHER:

Yours of May 30th came this evening, and as we are likely to move to-morrow morning I take this opportunity to write a few lines. We came here day before yesterday, and were informed we

would possibly remain here several days, and our men cleaned up
the camp to-day. We are about twenty-five miles from Atlanta.
We expect to be in possession of that place by the 4th of July,
though I think we will have to fight a hard battle before then.
We have a very large force now—sufficient, it is believed to
flank any position the enemy shall take, as we have been doing
since our advance from Ringgold. We have, of course, lost many
men, though I think we receive reinforcements sufficient to keep
up our original strength. The rebs are, undoubtedly, making desperate efforts, and they show wonderful pluck. There is very little
farming going on in this country—not even enough will be raised
to sustain the home population, if any were at home, but they are
not; the whole country is deserted. Wheat will not amount to a
quarter of a crop, and very little corn is planted.

Your affectionate son, HENRY.

CAMP NEAR MARIETTA, GA., June 16th, 1864.
DEAR FATHER:

We are still in line of battle, though our division has been in
reserve for the past four days. We suffered so heavily on the 27th,
that we may be favored in the next fight. I wrote to sister that our
loss would reach a thousand, on the 27th, but it proves to be nearer
1500, and mostly the work of an hour. We are driving the rebels
very slowly. Picket firing was kept up last night, all night, quite
heavy, but it has slackened a good deal this morning. Our artillery keeps shelling them constantly, but can get no reply. They are
said to be short of ammunition, and as we drive them we find evidences of masked batteries, which looks a little as if they had been
setting traps for us, and did not like to expose their position. Our
Generals are moving very cautiously however. Deserters say the
rebel General Polk was killed by one of our shells a day or two ago.
I made out a semi-monthly report of Company F this morning, and
find the aggregate number only fifty-one. Dead and discharged,
forty-five—in less than two years. It looks as if but few of us will
be left if the war continues another year.

This has been a tedious campaign, and don't seem near over.
This country is almost an entire wilderness, though not quite so
hilly as it has been.

We have had rain for eight days in succession, but it cleared up day before yesterday.

Men and officers are neraly naked and getting lousy. Have had no soap for more than two weeks, and no opportunity to wash clothes, save in cold water, since we left Cleveland, May 2d, and no prospect of any until this campaign is over, which will not be until we get to Atlanta.

The nomination of Mr. Lincoln was expected by us all, and very little comment is made. His vote in the army will depend very much on the success of Grant and Sherman. Their failure will divide the vote if a war Democrat is nominated. McClellan has many friends here, and will get a large vote if nominated and he repudiates Vallandigham and his party.

NEAR MARIETTA, GA., June 21st, 1864.

DEAR FATHER :

We are gradually approaching Marietta, although the rebels still occupy it and seem very determined in their defense.

The last line of works we drove them from, which was day before yesterday, they showed more signs of demoralization than ever before. Our regiment had skirmished with them until they were driven into their works on the 17th. On the 18th we harrassed them so with artillery and musketry that they left in the night, and we picked up more prisoners in the morning than at any other time—some seventy-five in our brigade front alone. They only fell back about one and a half miles, where they are now, but they get no rest.

It rains all the time, but nothing seems to check Sherman. He never gets mud-bound. He has been called crazy. If the same crazy kind of soldiering had been practiced long ago the result would have been peace before this.

There is considerable sickness, principally the result of such hard service, and not serious, only needing rest to bring them up again. I had thirty-three men for duty when I left Ringgold ; eighteen this morning, though seven of the number were lost in the fight of May 27th

The mail boy has just handed me yours of June 12th, with sister's enclosed. I am glad to hear such good account of things in the "Promised Land," and only wish I was there to see it, but almost begin to despair.

The roar of musketry and artillery is constant day and night, and often terrific. It is not uncommon for us to change our position two or three times a day. The fighting is generally late in the evening, continuing often away into the night, to secure positions, and then breastworks to build before morning. The rebels and we have built breastworks enough since we commenced this campaign to make a continuous line more than 100 miles long. For some reason they fire much less than we do, especially artillery. Prisoners say they are short of ammunition. We have seen cartridges manufactured in June, 1864, which would indicate as much. Should we gain a decided victory over them before we are worn out I think General Sherman is the man to follow it up.

Could you see us as we are this morning you would consider us (officers and all) as objects of charity. A dirtier or more ragged set you never beheld. Our living consists of hard bread, bacon and coffee. I would willingly give five dollars for a peck of potatoes, but they are an impossibility at present.

Rebel camps show evidences of scarcity. No remnants are scattered about as formerly; nothing but an occasional piece of corn bread and grains of corn, where they have fed their horses, which they seem to have plenty of yet. They appear to be out of meat as no bones or refuse pieces are found.

With love to all, your son,   HENRY.

NEAR MARIETTA, GA., June 22d, 1864.

DEAR FATHER:

Yours of 12th received, and I wrote you quite a long letter, enclosed it in an envelope, and put it in my memorandum-book without sealing, ready for the mail. About 2 P. M. we were ordered suddenly to advance, and in the little dash we made at the Rebs I lost my book and the letter. We drove the enemy a short distance, but they are very stubborn. They have a line of works on every ridge, which are from a quarter to a mile apart. We take more prisoners each time we advance. Yesterday the skirmish line in front of Willich's brigade fired one shot and threw away their arms and came into our lines. They were Tennessee troops principally, the first we have seen since this campaign begun. They are not considered reliable by the rebel commanders, and are rarely placed in the front. It rains every day regularly, but nothing seems to stop Sherman. It is a continual fusilade from morning to night, and night to morning. I think we fire fifty shots where they fire one. They are probably short of ammunition. Your affectionate son,

HENRY.

CAMP NEAR MARIETTA, GA., June 28th, 1864.
DEAR FATHER :

Nothing new since my last, only General Newton's Division of our corps made a charge, and were repulsed with considerable loss. We were marched out, leaving everything behind save our guns and haversacks, and expected a general engagement : but when Newton was repulsed we were ordered back to camp. I sent you an Atlanta paper, which one of my men got on picket this morning. The rifle pits of the pickets are only a few yards apart, and though it is forbidden the men to have any intercourse with the enemy, the weather is so hot that both parties are too indolent or too weary to shoot : and when the officers are not watching, the men on both sides get talking, and will meet each other half-way, and trade tobacco, coffee, papers, etc., and have a chat, but a shot from either of the lines near them causes them to scamper back to the rifle pits in double-quick time. No more at present. Your son,

HENRY.

CAMP IN THE FIELD,
NEAR MARIETTA, GA., July 3d, 1864.

The rebels evacuated their position last night, and we are ready and waiting orders to follow them. I visited their works about daylight this morning, and witnessed the most sickening sight I have seen during the war. Immediately in front of the works which we moved to last night, and previously occupied by the Fourteenth Corps, there had been two successive charges by the rebels and one by our men about a week ago. The rebels were allowed to get within ten feet of the works before a gun was fired. The effects of the firing then were terrible. The dead still lay on the top of the ground in heaps—many of them falling against the embankment. Neither party dared to leave their works to bury them. Probably they thought that the stench would drive our men from their position. It was awful, and had they not left last night we would have had to endure it as it was immediately in our front. That you may judge the number of shots fired, the top logs of their works, generally about eight inches through, were entirely shot away, so that it was necessary to put on new ones, and large chestnut trees, that screened their sentinels, were wilting from the effects of bullets.

In front of their works they had guards made by taking a sapling and boring two rows of two inch holes, with sharpened stakes through them a few inches apart ; also, sharpened stakes projecting from their works. It was the strongest position, and best fortified, I have yet seen, and if we did not outnumber them largely, which enables us to flank them, they could not have been taken.

2 P. M.—We have halted for dinner south of Marietta. Heavy cannonading in front—perhaps four or five miles. All sorts of rumors afloat, one of which is, that our cavalry is in Atlanta, and infantry across the river. It is premature, I think.

My congratulations to Mrs. M. when you see her.

While you were enjoying the marriage feast, on the evening of the 23d, I was groping in the darkness, after the fight, looking up wounded and dead men of our regiment. Your son. HENRY.

CAMP NINETY-THIRD O. V. I..
ON CHATTAHOOCHEE RIVER. July 11th, 1864.

DEAR FATHER :

We moved four or five miles yesterday up the river, and I suppose will cross to-day. The Twenty-third. and part of our corps. are already across.

We hoped when the rebels crossed the river the campaign would end for the present ; but no sooner had they evacuated their works on this side night before last. crossed and burned the railroad bridge. than we were on the march.

We now constitute a part of what the rebels call Sherman's Flanking Machine.

The work of the army is very unequally divided, and I think Thomas is very partial to the Fourteenth Corps, giving them all post and garrison duty and less of the fighting than any other corps in this Department. There is much grumbling among officers and men on this account, and when this campaign does end there will be more resignations offered than ever before from this corps. When General Baird's Division relieved us yesterday the feeling was manifested by the men calling them Thomas' pets, and saying there's no danger here boys; hold this position till we drive them away again, and build works, and then you can move up again. The boys will have their joke! Your son.   HENRY.

CAMP, CHATTAHOOCHEE RIVER, July 14th, 1864.

DEAR SISTER:

Yours of 6th, dated at Elland, came safely to hand.

We expected to make a reconnoisance in force to-day, but the order has been countermanded, and I devote a part of the day to you.

We are now on the south side of the river, and can see Atlanta from our camp, distant ten or twelve miles. Looking over the country it seems to be covered with heavy timber.

There has been unusual quiet along the whole line for several days, and but little resistance offered to our crossing the river. It seems strange after such a stubborn resistance at all other points.

I received a letter from brother George a few days ago, and am not surprised to learn that he would be glad to be home again, and I think a hundred days will effectually cure him of soldiering, and do hope he may pass safely through. The greatest danger is in the first battles, as he will not know how to take advantage of positions and screen himself, but it is more than probable that he will not get into a fight.

Political affairs north don't look encouraging and financial matters no better. You may think I am becoming less patriotic; perhaps I am. Two years of such service and such results certainly has a tendency that way. When I became satisfied that the administration had adopted the policy of universal emancipation, without qualification, in the s.ceded States. I felt that it had undertaken a contract which could not be carried out, and should Mr. Lincoln be defeated, it will undoubtedly be canceled. A man of the Vallandigham stamp can't be elected; but some other shrewder and less objectionable Democrat, that will prove equally as dangerous, may be. But you must excuse all this. Our vision, out here in Dixie, may not be a very broad and clear one; but still we must look, though we do not see much perhaps.

I guess father thinks because I was scarce of paper once that I am all the time, for he sends me a sheet in every letter he writes. As ever, your affectionate brother,   HENRY.

POWERS' FERRY,
CHATTAHOOCHEE RIVER, July 18th, 1864.
DEAR FATHER:

We have been resting a few days, but are ready this morning for a forward movement.

Yesterday our division went down the river about four miles and assisted the Fourteenth Corps in crossing. There was but little opposition offered.

The rebels are said to be about four miles in our front intrenched, which I suppose we will know more about before night.

The final struggle for Atlanta cannot be very far distant. I have no doubt of ultimate success, but don't know at what sacrifice.

I received a letter from brother George. I judge one hundred days will cure him of soldiering. It is just long enough for him to become heartily disgusted. A longer term he would become more reconciled and like it better.   HENRY RICHARDS.

BEFORE ATLANTA, August 13th, 1864.
DEAR FATHER:

I believe the last date I received of yours is July 23d. You speak of taking a $1,000 Court House bond. I wish I could send my money home, but we have not been paid for nearly eight months, and when we are paid I presume we will only get paid for four.

We have no use for money here, as there is nothing to buy save tobacco, and as I only smoke, a very little does me. We have had easy times since we have been here, and not much exposed to danger. Occasionally a sixty-four pound shot is dropped in our lines, but it rarely does any harm, and only causes the men to shout a defiance. There is scarcely a moment that the heavy boom of cannon is not heard somewhere on the line, and the picket firing is incessant. Our regiment is on picket every six days, and fires about 8,000 rounds in the twenty-four hours, at a cost of about $136 to the gover ment. The length of line we occupy is about 300 yards. The whole line is not less than ten or twelve miles long. The heaviest fighting is on the extreme right. We are making an occasional demonstration to attract their attention. We have news of the capture of Mobile, which is good if true.   * *

Should any accident befall me, I suppose some one will be kind enough to acquaint you with it, though everything here is just like business at home. No one makes any particular preparation for disaster here any more than there. Perhaps I may be singular, for I have felt confident in every engagement that I would get through all right, and I don't like to admit of a doubt now by making any requests. Maybe I am a little superstitious: if such *is* the case, I can't help it. I am acting on a court-martial now, and if we were at Atlanta I presume I should be very pleasantly situated, as it may last for several weeks. Your son,   HENRY.

BEFORE ATLANTA, GA., August 25th, 1864.

DEAR FATHER:

We are preparing to move, but have no positive orders. The court-martial I was on were ordered to adjourn, and the artillery is being drawn off from the front. I know nothing of the extent or direction of the move, but as fifteen days' rations and forage are ordered, I presume we are to cut loose from our base, but Sherman knows his business, and I have faith in his plans, and I heartily endorse his sentiments in the enclosed letter. How any man can satisfy his conscience and sense of duty by securing as his substitute an ignorant black man, taken from the southern plantations, when the very life of his country and friends is at stake, is more than I can understand.

We are now, I think, approaching the most critical period of the war. Our armies are being reduced by expiration of terms of service; a Presidential election, with rather more than its usual excitement; a draft to be enforced, together with wide-spread dissatisfaction, encouraged by a large party at the North, and who, in many places, are boldly advising open resistance to the enforcement of the laws—cause us fellows out in the front to think very seriously of affairs. We have had some experience in soldiering now, and know we can hold our own, and our eyes are turned to the North. There is really where this battle is being fought. A loyal spirit manifested there by the people to the government and this army, will give us renewed energy; and, with John Brown's spirit, the army will be ever found marching on.

We have just received orders to withdraw at midnight, and I must close. I would like your opinion at length on the present state of affairs at home. I must confess I feel uneasy, but really hope my fears are unfounded, and that our people at home, taking the army as their guide, will rally around the flag, and give the soldiers their undivided support. There is only one way out of this thing, and that is by the overthrow of the Rebellion. The people of the North must see this, and act accordingly, or they and the whole country are gone. As ever, your son. HENRY.

ATLANTA, GA., September 25th, 1864.

DEAR FATHER:

Yours from Iowa was received yesterday. I have not written home since we arrived at Atlanta.

We are pleasantly situated about three miles out on the road to Augusta, with no rebs in our front, at least none to hurt.

There is nothing new here, and no movement is likely for some time yet, I presume.

We have just received the news of Sheridan's victories, which is glorious news; also an order to make out pay rolls for eight months, which is also good news, as we are flat broke.

I was notified a few days ago that I would be sent, with other officers to clean out and bring up men who are in hospitals and are fit for duty. There are many kept there by officers, because they want a command, and if the wards are not kept full the camp and hospital is broken up, and they will be obliged to go to the front, and many of them prefer that their duty should " take any shape but that," hence they will not send one man away until another comes to take his place. If I am sent my duties may take me as far north as Cleveland, O., and I may be able to give you a flying visit.

I have an application ready to forward asking for a change of duty during the fall and winter months, as I feel that I shall not be able to stand a winter campaign. If not successful in that I shall be compelled, I fear, to offer my resignation, as my health is failing fast. Your son, HENRY.

BIG SHANTY, October 15th, 1864.

DEAR SISTER:

It seems an age since I have heard from home. Communication has been so interrupted of late that we begin to despair of getting another mail, but we have just been notified that a mail would go out at 3 o'clock—it is now 2 P. M.—and that we may expect a mail to-morrow.

It will be several days before the railroad is fully repaired, it having been pretty effectually destroyed for many miles. We left Atlanta on the 2d to head off the rebs and prevent the destruction of the road, but were one day too late. We are now about twenty-four miles north of Atlanta, and will remain about here until the road is finished.

My health is still very poor. I called on General Wood about ten days ago and showed my certificates from our surgeon and asked his approval to my application for a change of duty during fall and winter. He was very polite, but advised me not to think of doing so, and said if he was in my condition he would tender his resignation at once ; and I believe I will. I am not sanguine of its being accepted, however, as I know of one being returned from an officer who had equally as strong a certificate as I can get.

Hoping to-morrow's mail may contain letters from home for me, I am, as ever, your affectionate brother, HENRY.

OFFICERS' HOSPITAL,
LOOKOUT MOUNTAIN, October 20th, 1864.

DEAR SISTER:

I merely write to let you know where I am, as I wrote a few days ago from the regiment saying I was not well. I did not think I would be in the hospital so soon, nor would I, but all convalescents and sick, not fit for duty, both biped and quadruped, were ordered to Chattanooga, and you may well believe we made the sorriest looking caravan that was ever seen from this army. We were sent without any guards, for Sherman well knew Hood nor any of his commands would not care to take us. I am very tired and literally worn out, otherwise I don't feel as poorly as I did when I wrote you last.

The army has turned southward, after following Hood within ten miles of Tunnel Hill, and Lord knows when Sherman will stop his pursuit. It is the intention to subsist the army upon the country. Sherman has the entire confidence of the men, and is certainly a man of rare ability, and makes but few pretensions. Has no staff, or at least I have never seen more than one officer with him at a time, and looks *military* about as much as father would, and rides a horse as carelessly. I should be glad if we had more generals as crazy as he.

I forgot to say I left the army the 18th and arrived here to day.

Hoping to hear from you soon, your affectionate brother.

HENRY.

OFFICERS' HOSPITAL,
LOOKOUT MOUNTAIN, November 1st, 1864.

DEAR SISTER:

Yours of the 25th received day before yesterday. I intended writing father yesterday, but was so occupied in watching our corps as it came into the valley below us that I did not get time. I have not learned where they are going, but rumor says to guard the railroad between Stephenson and Athens. If so, I think I will try and go with them, although I am not fit for active field service. Still I would rather do garrison duty than stay here. This is a most beautiful place, commanding the grandest views, and an excellent place for very sick men, but convalescents would enjoy a little more life, such as is plainly visible below; but I must not complain. It is, I know, the best the Government can do for us. I go before the medical board this afternoon for examination: was before them last Monday, but a decision has been deferred until to-day. They seem to think it strange I have never been in the hospital before, and, I suppose, had I shirked duty more, and had a better hospital record, it would be an advantage to me in their eyes. It appears very difficult for truth and honesty to get a hearing, and when I come to think of it, it is not very remarkable. The doctor attending me is a very good physician, and a gentleman in every way. I take only simple remedies. He suggested *Croton* oil, but I objected, and he did not insist, and this morning asked if I would take cod liver oil. I told him I would try it. But I could only hand it to the nurse, and tell him to say to the doctor that it or I must leave the room, as the smell was more than I could stand. A lieutenant occupies the room with me, who has been suffering for more than a year, and unfit for duty most of the time. He has offered his resignation time and again, but, until recently, without avail: but since I came here it has been accepted, but alas! too late; poor fellow, he can live but a few days. But it is nearly time for me to appear before the wise men, and I must close. Don't think of coming here to me, as it could be of no use, and exceeding difficult for you. As ever. your affectionate brother,

HENRY.

Captain Richards finally succeeded in obtaining his discharge December 27th, 1864, and returned home, a broken-down and worn-out man. He had always been subject to bronchial troubles, and the exposure of the last two years wore out a constitution, seemingly strong, but in which consumption was an hereditary malady.

He returned to the old homestead, at Elland, and after various stages of hopefulness and doubt, sank at last to rest, on the 18th of August, 1865, and was buried in the family cemetery, at Elland.

To his acquaintances and friends, for whom more particularly this compilation is made, nothing need be said by way of eulogy of Henry Richards.

> " Little did he crave
> " Men's praises. Modestly, with kindly mirth,
> " Not sad nor bitter, he accepted fate,—
> " Drank deep of life, knew books and hearts of men,
> " Cities and camps and war's immortal woe ;
> " Yet bore through all (such virtue in him sate
> " His spirit is not whiter now than then !)
> " A simple, loyal nature, pure as snow."